LEMURIA
∇ ∇ ∇

Lemuria

THE LOST CONTINENT OF THE PACIFIC

By WISHAR S. CERVÉ

with a Special Chapter

By DR. JAMES D. WARD

ROSICRUCIAN LIBRARY
VOLUME XII

SAN JOSE, CALIFORNIA

ROSICRUCIAN PRESS

Printing and Publishing Dept.

AMORC COLLEGE

FIRST EDITION, SEPTEMBER 1931

Printed in U. S. A.

ROSICRUCIAN PRESS
San Jose, California

DEDICATION

▽ ▽ ▽

*In appreciation of the first researches
into the history of the lost
continents of*

ATLANTIS AND LEMURIA,

*made by that brilliant
mind and soul,*

SIR FRANCIS BACON

*this book is dedicated to his memory and
everlasting greatness of character.*

THE AUTHOR

THE ROSICRUCIAN LIBRARY

▽ ▽ ▽

VOLUME

I. Rosicrucian Question and Answers with Complete History of the Order.

II. Rosicrucian Principles for the Home and Business.

III. Mystical Life of Jesus.

IV. The Secret Doctrines of Jesus.
(In preparation.)

V. "Unto Thee I Grant"
(Secret Teachings of Tibet.)

VI. A Thousand Years of Yesterdays.
(A Revelation of Reincarnation.)

VII. Self Mastery and Fate with the Cycles of Life.

VIII. Rosicrucian Manual.

IX. Mystics at Prayer.

X. Rosicrucian Healing.

XI. Mansions of the Soul.
(The Cosmic Conception.)

XII. Lemuria, The Lost Continent of the Pacific.

*(Other volumes will be added from time to time.
Write for complete Catalogue.)*

CONTENTS

▽ ▽ ▽

Publishers' Preface

Some years ago a representative of the Rosicrucian Brotherhood in China visited our offices
in San Francisco and placed in our hands, as an of-
ficial portfolio, some very rare manuscripts dealing
with many of the age-old traditions preserved in
the secret archives of Tibet and China. Among
these manuscripts was a very old and worn copy
of the secret spiritual and ethical teachings of the
Tibetans, which this representative was anxious
to have brought to light in the Western World in
modern form. The truly mystical and private
manuscripts of a Rosicrucian nature were de-
posited with us for use in connection with our
usual activities as publishers of the magazines and
other printed matter of the Rosicrucian Brotherhood.

In order to facilitate the proper publication and
public dissemination of the Tibetan teachings the
foreign representative organized a publishing com-
pany under the name of the *Oriental Literature*

Syndicate, and this syndicate produced the Tibetan manuscript in book form under the title of "Unto Thee I Grant—" This rare book has had a number of editions and is considered one of the most beautiful specimens of Oriental literature published in recent years.

Among the manuscripts retained by the *Oriental Literature Syndicate* were several dealing with the ancient records and traditions telling the story of the lost continent of Lemuria. It was the intention of the *Syndicate* eventually to gather together from all parts of the world the thousands of tabulated and recorded facts regarding Lemuria and its people, and to put these into a highly instructive and fascinating book for public dissemination. The work of gathering this information and compiling it was placed in the hands of Wishar Spenle Cervé, who was selected because of his interest in the subjects of archaeology, geology, and meteorology. As the matter was gradually accumulated and the astonishing facts put into readable form, many interesting stories evolved, each of which was worthy of independent publication. One of these stories was published by us in the Rosicrucian magazine known as "The Mystic Triangle" for August 1925. The publication of this story aroused wide spread interest and immediately there were requests from all parts of the world for the further publication of similar stories or the publication of a complete book dealing exhaustively with Lemuria and its people.

With the assistance of representatives in China and Tibet, the entire holdings of the Oriental Literature Syndicate were taken over by the publishing department of the Rosicrucian Brotherhood in America, and therefore the book called "Unto Thee I Grant—" and all the other accumulated manuscripts and records owned by the Syndicate became the possession of the Rosicrucian Brotherhood of AMORC for North America.

The researches started by Mr. Cervé have continued during the past ten years, and because of the increasing demand for the publication of the fascinating facts, we decided to have him put the most essential ones and the most alluring parts of the story of Lemuria into a public book, free from all technical data of a ponderous nature, and replete with the human interest features which make the story of Lemuria the equal of any of the world's fascinating romances.

This book is now offered in the present form with the hope that it will please and instruct as well as satisfy the natural curiosity in the minds of millions of persons living in the Western World.

To a great many the book will be a surprising revelation, and undoubtedly thousands of readers will question the truthfulness of all the facts stated herein and will demand scientific proof and verification. A complete index of all of the records, writings, traditions and facts regarding Lemuria would make a book of itself. We have deemed it advisable to state a few of these authorities and records in an appendix to this book, but we do not attempt to establish the facts of Lemuria in such a manner as to be indisputably verified in the minds of those who would undoubtedly question any or all of the statements regardless of what proof might be submitted. There are certain facts that are self-evident regarding Lemuria, and its people, and these few or many, as the readers may discover them, constitute a selection or framework throughout the present volume that is sufficient foundation upon which to build a firm belief in the entire story. To ignore these indisputable facts and self-evident points and criticize a few which have not been substantiated by the most acceptable authorities is to do an injustice to the work of the author.

We have just stated that our desire has been to make this book free from ponderous, scientific quotations, and for any to take advantage of this by criticizing the lack of such evidence will be a sign of insincerity. If the self-evident and indisputable facts to be found in this book are given proper consideration, there can be no doubt left in the mind of any critic that most of the entire story of Lemuria as recorded herein must be true.

One of the points that might be disputed is in connection with the statement that the changes which have occurred on the surface of the earth in past centuries have been in cycles. Many years ago this astonishing fact was discovered by a well-known scientist, Mr. John H. Tice. When he attempted to publish his findings in 1875 no publisher would accept his statements of the scientific principles constituting natural evidences of a

Cosmic power and the manifestation of Cosmic laws unknown to other scientists. He, therefore, published his findings in private form and we are happy to quote part of these findings in support of the claim for cycles of changes in the earth's surface in *Appendix Number One* at the close of this book. Much that Mr. Tice published privately in 1875 and practically all that is contained in his rare manuscripts now in our possession have been verified in recent years by the independent researches of hundreds of other scientists, none of whom, however, have so completely related the various discoveries and strange manifestations as Mr. Tice related them in outlining his theory.

The people of the Western World seem to be generally of the opinion that outside of sacred literature very little positive information regarding ancient times is available or of a dependable nature. It is common belief, for instance, that the only complete or authentic record of any great flood, which, as a cataclysm, destroyed or changed part of the earth's surface is to be found in the sacred writings now published in the form of the Bible or in related Jewish records. The truth of the matter is that this great flood and many others are very completely and interestingly recorded in the sacred and scientific records of many ancient peoples, and verification of these are found in the modern records of nature's own archaeological registry.

From similar writings and records of the ancients the facts contained in this book have been gathered and compiled without discrimination, and without religious or scientific bias.

We wish to acknowledge our appreciation for valuable help and assistance to the many persons mentioned in our appendix relating to authorities, and especially to Dr. Ward for his special chapter dealing with the very unique subject with which he is most intimate as a high representative and gradu-ate of some of the oldest institutions of learning in India.

The American people, especially those living in California, will be delighted with the mysterious facts contained in this book and we feel sure that all those living in North and South America, and who are citizens of these countries will feel a great-er pride in the ancestry and origin of their coun-tries and their native races. We feel that this book

LEMURIA

has a glorious message and a means for much en-
joyment in the field of fascinating research.

THE PUBLISHERS—

INTRODUCTION

I wish to anticipate many comments that will be made regarding this book by those who may have expected to find within its covers a scientific treatise on the subject. I have not attempted to make this book a treatise on the subjects of anthropology or anthropometry, nor in the fields of archaeological and geological research. Nor will meteorologists, astronomers, cosmologists or others find herein a ponderous encyclopedia of technical information.

With the same enormous mass of facts which I have had at my disposal, and with the same artists and other assistants ready and qualified to prepare matter in a technical form for me, such a book as some may anticipate could have been prepared and offered to the public, or to that limited portion of the public, desiring its knowledge in a technical form. But my purpose was to comply with the desires of the publishers in preparing and presenting an easily readable, enjoyable, and fascinating account of the lost Continent of Lemuria, with all of its past history, effects upon the races of man, and ancient, human incidents of life.

After all, it is a fact that all of us enjoy a relaxation from preachments and ponderous academic dissertations no matter how deeply we may be concerned with specialized scientific subjects. The very men who claim to cast aside a book that deals lightly with an historical, learned, or scientific subject are found in their times of relaxation completely lost and absorbed in the fascinating and alluring stories of the popular magazines and Sunday newspapers; and I do not hesitate to say that I have found among my scientific acquaintances many who have admittedly discovered their first clues to attractive subjects of research through the reading of the semi-scientific articles prepared for lay reading in the popular publications

Scientific research and investigation may be substantial food to the scientific mind, but a readable story, brilliantly coloring the human interest side of the facts revealed by science, never fails to become food to the emotional, human, side of our natures.

The facts contained in this volume are arranged and presented in the same manner that the facts of life are presented to you daily. The serious points are mingled with those that are amusing or lightly interesting, instructive, or perhaps practical. The beam of the spotlight of interest is centered more upon the human-interest features of the story than upon the ponderous technicalities of scientific erudition. The people, the characters, the scenes in the backgrounds, the facts and figures themselves, are all brought out of their laboratory niches and heavily draped positions, and paraded upon the stage of life before us to the accompaniment of lively music with the bright lights playing upon them while we, the readers in the audience, watch this age-old play of life go on and on.

The story in this volume is a play of life that started over two hundred thousand years ago with a vague and indefinite prologue, and continuing through many astonishing, surprising, interesting, acts up to the present time. The play is still going on, for the descendants of Lemuria are still in our midst, and we are daily contacting the effects produced by these people who attained a high degree

of civilization and established many principles of
life which are still fixed in their purpose and
practice.

After my task was started and I had overcome
the hesitancy I had in writing lightly and freely in
a non-technical manner of matters that might have
been dealt with more deeply, I began to enjoy the
work. I found the continents of which I was
writing becoming alive, instead of dead, specimens
painted on old yellow maps. The people themselves looked at me, talked to me, and told me their
stories, and I found myself entering into their
communities and observing the transitions in nature, the changes in all forms of life, and the evolution of the races of man. Then it was I discovered why the facts of the story of the lost continent of Lemuria had never reached a universal
understanding among the lay-minds of the public.
Only the geologists, archaeologists, profound his-
torians and those who delve into the anthropology
of man have found any interest in the history of
Lemuria, and what they found they tabulated in
such a dry and uninteresting manner and preserved as such sacred personal assets of their own

achievements in research, that few knew what had actually been discovered.

I hope, therefore, that this book will make the subject more popular and arouse further interest in the investigation of the hundreds of available sources of information still untouched by those who have spent their lifetime seeking for positive facts.

With this hope and with the further desire that what I have written may contribute to a better understanding of the development of the human individual in all of his physical, mental, spiritual, and so-called psychic qualities, I offer this work.

W. S. C.

July 7, 1931.

▽ ▽ ▽

Chapter I.

THE FIRST RACES OF MAN IN AMERICA

ONE of the most interesting problems in the study of world civilization is the origin of the first races of men in America.

It has been commonly believed, as a popular idea, that the cradle of civilization was in Mesopotamia and there is a very general belief that the first races of man could be traced to some Oriental country. In fact, the so-called *Garden of Eden* has always been considered as a mythical description of an Oriental location.

A few years ago some scientists advanced the idea that the valley of the Ohio River might have been the real Garden of Eden, inasmuch as discoveries there tended to indicate that the mound builders and the cave dwellers may have descended from the first races of man to people the earth, and various relics unearthed in that valley seemed to be older than anything that had been found up to the

period of their discovery. Since then further discoveries have changed the idea somewhat. While
it is generally admitted that there is ample evidence
to prove that the Ohio Valley did shelter and pro-
tect some races of man antedating the history of
man in many other parts of the world, there are
now many evidences to indicate that the Pacific
Coast of the United States is unquestionably the
only existing location of the earliest races of men
who had reached a civilized state of development.

Many and various fantastic theories have been
given to account for the presence of the aboriginal
Americans. The history of the origin of the American Indian is a wonderful study and is a subject
which may never be completely cleared of its
mysteries.

The fact that the American Indians were divid-
ed into many tribes widely separated in their lo-
cations and widely differing in their language and
yet appearing very much alike and having many
customs and habits in common, permit of many
forms of speculation as to their origin. The things
which have been found to be common with most
of the American Indian tribes afford a foundation

for the theory that all of them were descendants of one race, while the many differences in their habits and customs and in their language afford a foundation for the theory that they were in no way related and that those in the western part of North America may have descended from other races that came from the West, while those in the eastern part of the continent were descendants of Eastern tribes or races who had made early contact with this continent.

In studying the problem we have many reliable scientific principles as guides and much data of an accumulative nature that constitutes a fairly dependable index. In studying the history of men we must bear in mind that there are certain characteristics which are common to all races and that slight variation may not always indicate distinct races but rather the effect of environment upon countenances, nature, and habits of man.

Certainly, we are face to face with one of the two possible explanations for the existence of the many races of man. Either all the races of man throughout the world had one common origin, in one cradle, in one location, and from this one point moved in all directions to cover the face of the earth, or man had his origin in many places throughout the world practically simultaneously. The question therefore is whether all mankind had one common origin and became differentiated in races and characteristics through evolution affected by environment as man moved to various parts of the world, or whether human beings evolved or were created in hundreds of widely scattered localities at the same time with distinct characteristics, natures, and habits in accordance with the purpose of creation and the environment in which the creation occurred.

Environment and the consequential effects of it will change the nature, appearance, habits, and customs of any race and it is perfectly possible for all of the races of man to have had one common origin and to have been identical in countenance, customs, and habits until the members of this one original race became scattered in various parts of the world and developed future generations having such modifications as the effect of environment would produce.

We know that men who live where there is an abundance of bright light such as in the northern or southern polar regions or in countries having wide areas of snow for many months of the year, or where there is a great amount of white sand reflecting the brilliant sunlight, acquire squinting eyes or eyes which become slightly oblique, and from the squinting and continuous attempt to keep the eyes partly closed against the glaring light the cheek bones have a tendency to be raised or the muscles of the face are raised to appear like high cheek bones. On the other hand, those who live in the mountains or mountainous regions and must climb a great deal and struggle much in moving from place to place, soon develop strong legs, deep chests and powerfully developed muscles in the back, and these characteristics are transmitted from generation to generation until we have a different type of man from those living where there is snow or desert lands.

Likewise, the races of men who live along rivers or the borders of oceans and have developed means of moving rafts or logs or other floating things for conveyances, using the arms as a motive power rather than the legs, soon develop broad chests and powerful shoulders with great muscular arms and under-developed legs.

Just these few points will indicate to you how physical characteristics may be developed in successive generations until an almost distinct race of man may be evolved through the effects of environment. If we add to these effects the additional ones of deeply tanned complexion in the warmer or brilliantly lighted climates or where there is a great deal of sunlight as in the north and south polar regions, and fairer complexions in the mountains or shaded valley sections of the temperate zones, and the effect upon the height and physical development generally resulting from warm or cold climates, accompanied by the effect upon the thickness, color and growth of the hair on the body, we will see that many greatly modified and diversified forms of the human body will evolve under the effects of environment.

We must not forget, either, the effect of food, water, and personal habits. The mental development of a race, adding to it the character of the soul within, also has an extremely important ef-

fect upon the outer appearance of man. It is generally conceded that the more intelligent races of
man developed in those countries where the climate
was extremely mild or cold while the less intelligent
races developed in those countries where there was
extreme heat. Analyzing this we find a very
logical reason for this law. In the colder countries
where there is much snow and ice man was forced
to invent and reason out ways and means of clothing himself and protecting himself against the cold
and the winds and he had to invent homes and
shelter, and devise ways and means of warming
them. He had to devise ways and means of secur-
ing food and preserving it. All this taxed his
imagination, challenged his mental ability, and
made him more industrious and a deeper thinker.
Those who lived in the very mild and warmer
climates found an abundance of food the year
around, required little or no clothing, no specially
constructed homes or huts of any kind, and because of the heat and the enervating effects of the
climate he became sluggish in his thinking and in
his physical actions.

There are some modifications to the above and there are some indications of races that reached a high degree of culture in tropical climates, but most of these modifications are explained by the fact that those parts of the world that are now tropical may not have always been so tropical and those places which are now so completely covered with snow may have been more temperate in climate; and again many of the races of man that attained high civilization in tropical lands were descendants of tribes that came to such countries from more temperate or colder zones.

In so far as North America is concerned it is a remarkable fact that all of the explorations and investigations into the antiquity and origin of the primitive races of this continent show that the greatest and highest degree of civilization was attained on the Pacific coast. I will speak more of this later, but in passing it may be fitting to say here that this is an important point in our consideration of the history and ultimate disappearance of the continent of Lemuria and the distribution of its surviving people.

In considering whether the races of man had one common origin or not we must keep in mind the fact that if the races of man originated in one locality and from that point distributed their descendants throughout the world, we must concede that there were ways and means for the journeying of the races of men from one continent to another throughout the world. In this regard we have little difficulty for there is every indication of a reliable nature, that many of the great open spaces now filled with oceans and bodies of water were at one time occupied by continents and large islands.

We need not resort to the theoretical possibility of man having travelled from Russia and through Asia across the Bering Strait into Alaska, for while there is evidence that men of an Asiatic origin did eventually reach Alaska and leave monuments there proving the fact, nevertheless, there is other evidence to indicate that men reached the shores of America by devious routes in various ages.

On the other hand, in considering the question as to whether man may have originated in various parts of the world simultaneously and without contact or knowledge of the existence of other races in other parts of the world, we have this one very important fact to keep in mind, namely, that investigations and researches including the most carefully made study of the relics found in excavations in all parts of the world show that the primitive or original races existing in each locality started with some culture or development of civilized ideas, and gradually created an original or independent civilization of its own. If all the races of man had one common origin and gradually spread throughout the world we must concede that the migrations would not have begun until man had attained a very high state of civilization and had developed many methods of caring for himself and promoting his best interests. In such a case those who reached foreign lands and established communities of their race on new and virgin soil where no other human beings had ever lived, would naturally have begun their new lives in a new land with a certain degree of advanced culture and advanced forms of civilization.

The rapidly accumulating evidence from all parts of the world proves that this is so. In nearly every case, the earliest relics, the earliest evidences of human occupation indicate some form of civilization and for this reason we have a right to assume that in these localities the races of men did not have their beginnings independent of any other races in any other parts of the world. Consideration must be given, of course, to the results of retrogression in culture in countries widely separated from easy contact with others.

There is a very large amount of evidence that proves conclusively that there was a considerable amount of migration in the early history of this earth. This is especially true of the Pacific coast, of South America, and is an important factor in the study of the mystery of the disappearance of the continent of Lemuria.

Before entering upon a discussion of the existence of the continent of Lemuria and a description of its people and their habits and customs it may be well to state in this first chapter the nature of some of the evidence that has been carefully compiled after being gathered by many men and in many expeditions, all of which I have followed with keen interest. In the first place, it is more than likely that we shall eventually find that the North American Indians are descendants of the "lost tribes of Israel." This belief has gradually developed in the minds of those who have made a careful study of the origin of the American Indians and of their languages, customs, habits, and early products. It may be interesting to my readers to know that one of the outstanding discoveries in this regard was the finding that in all of the various tribes of Indians in America there are certain words that are common to all, although slightly different in sound or symbol. A list of these words common to all of the tribes has shown that they were words which were identical with words used by the tribes known as the Israelites.

When one considers the unusual and enormous diversity of the languages and the tribes of North American Indians and the fact that tribes that lived very near each other were unable to understand each other or to communicate with each other in any form, then the existence of certain common words of an identical nature and meaning become highly significant. In the second place, it has been found that nearly all of these identical words had a religious or mystical meaning and had nothing to do with objects or conditions of a purely local nature, and very often related to principles and laws of a Cosmic nature and pertaining to nothing else in their language or in their customs and habits. In the third place, it was found that there were certain holidays or holy days or cere-monial days that were quite common to all of the tribes despite the great variance in their manner of living, their beliefs, and their tribal philosophy. Again it was found that most of these ceremonial days had a Cosmic, mystical and religious signi-ficance and were coincident with similar holy days prevalent among the "Israelites."

Again, considering the fact that many of these Indian tribes were so widely separated that an en-tire continent lay between them so that they were so unknown to each other that when they were eventually brought into contact with each other they were astounded to know of the existence of the other, we can well realize that the similarity and coincidence of ceremonial days could not be the result of late intercommunication or the recent exchange of ideas.

How the American Indians came to be the descendants of the "lost tribes of Israel" is a matter that requires further investigation and the presentation of the problem would require another separate book. The subject has no special relation-ship with our study of the continent of Lemuria except that we must keep in mind the fact that the American Indians may represent a portion of the descendants of Lemuria and Atlantis.

That these American Indians could have de-scended from the Israelites by way of migration across the Pacific is indicated by the fact that many Asiatic dialects and Asiatic evidences have been found in North America and this subject, too, is complete enough to constitute a volume of its own. But there is this significant point in con-nection with the study of the distribution of the Asiatic dialects and Asiatic distinctions. All of the Asiatic dialects and Asiatic relics are found only on the Pacific coast, and almost wholly along the north western shore of the North American continent. This becomes highly significant as we shall see later on.

On the other hand, along the western coast of
South America we find striking evidence of the
identity of tribal words with oceanic dialects,
plainly indicating and definitely proving that
there was some easy means of access between the
western shore of South America and the various
people of Oceania. In fact, many of the tribes
living along the western shore of South America
are surprisingly like the natives of many of the
present Pacific Islands both in features and color
and in many minute respects. For instance, the
Sirionos of Bolivia, constituting an isolated race of
primitive people unlike all of the other races of
that country but having slightly wavy hair of a
very fine texture with large bushy beards and
typical Oceanic features resembling no other race
anywhere in the world except those of Oceania,
are unlike any of the Indian tribes of either North
or South America. Furthermore, in some of the
expeditions which I have carefully followed and
worked with in analytical study of their researches,
there has been unearthed along the California coast
certain pre-historic graves in which were found
adzes, axe-heads, and other stone articles carefully

made, and in a style and manner typical of the work of some of the tribes still existing on islands in the Pacific Ocean, and made of stone that is found no where else except in those islands of the Pacific Ocean.

It must be kept in mind that these islands now existing in the Pacific are unquestionably the remnants of other islands and a large continent which once occupied the space or part of the space of the Pacific Ocean, and unless we concede that ancient men did sail or journey by some means for many months from distant islands in the Pacific to the western shore of South America, we must admit that there must have been other islands or large bodies of land in the Pacific close to South America and which were occupied by tribes like unto those still existing on the Pacific islands and with stone similar to that still found on such islands. In such a case it would have been a simple matter for the pre-historic tribes to have journeyed from the one continent on the Pacific to the other and to have made such migrations at a time when the Pacific continent was slowly submerging.

Another interesting point is the fact that North America affords the greatest study in the investigation of the origin of man because, even excluding the many American Indian tribes with their various dialects, customs, and habits, we still have evidence in North America of other tribes of distinctly different dialects and habits. In fact, the variation of races, of dialects, and customs, was unquestionably greater in this new world than it ever was in the old world, and so far as the Pacific coast is concerned, more than one hundred distinct languages or dialects were spoken by the various tribes within a few square miles, constituting a greater number of distinct tribes for the same amount of country than in any other part of this world. Even at the time that North America was first visited by explorers the condition of variation in tongue and character was highly impressive. Many of the natives were naked and savage; others were nomads. Other tribes were partly civilized. Some were agriculturists; some were hunters. Some dwelt in the open fields and valleys in the shelter of the brush and trees, while others had built their homes of adobe and the skins of animals using methods found in no other parts of the world, or using methods, customs, and habits that were identical with other tribes in other parts of the world. Most of the tribes evidenced a progressiveness in development to the stone age indicating that they had advanced beyond all the primitive states. Some of these tribes had already reached a very high state of culture and had attained real artistic skill, and many of them had accomplished feats which had never been excelled or equalled by any of the other races in the history of the world.

I am referring particularly to the Pacific coast where the early explorers were astonished to find among primitive races and primitive people the evidence of a very high civilization.

It is true that in the Yucatan there was found much evidence of a highly civilized race with a very remarkable development in culture, but this is the story of the Mayans, a race of people who descended from the Atlanteans and Lemurians intermarried, when the continent of Atlantis submerged in the Atlantic Ocean. This, too, is another story in the history of man that has no bearing upon the story of the Lemurians but the fact that the Mayan writing is one of the most marvelous achievements of any race and is known only in its most perfected form, and must have required thousands of years for development, indicates how a cultured and civilized race of people came to this North American continent to live among primitive conditions.

Certainly this gives us a picture of the polyglot of races of man, the mixtures of civilization, the variance of culture, and the wide dissemination of man himself on a continent in the new world, as it is called today, but which we shall see was really an old world before Europe had become even partly civilized.

In the book of Genesis we have a story of the origin of man that is not only symbolical but in some passages quite historical. We must bear in mind, however, that the story given to us in Genesis is the result of age-old traditions passed from person to person by word of mouth for many ages before becoming recorded in the crude writings on stones. Then such stories were later re-arranged and re-worded for preservation in manuscripts, and still later re-arranged, edited, and prepared for translation into other languages and for wider dissemination. The stories, therefore, of the origin of man and especially of the great flood, are not mythical stories but historical facts known to all ages of man as part of the traditions of man's history. Geology and the study of the earth's surface and a study of all of the things within the earth give us mute but indisputable evidence of the fact that at one time great floods did destroy most if not all of the living things on the face of the earth, and that as the flood came to various parts of the world there were migrations and the movement of hordes of people from one country to another. The flood was not simultaneous everywhere but gradual throughout a long period of time with one continent or another gradually disappearing here and there. There is scarcely a tribe of people in any part of the world that has not a story of a great flood among its traditions. The early visitors and explorers who came to the shores of America were astonished to find that the tribes living here in such great isolation and separated from all other parts of the world with no means of communication or contact with the traditions of the Orientals, had their own stories of a great flood that were identical with the stories told in Genesis and held by the people of Asia and other parts of the Orient. How this story of the world flood came to the American Indians and the hundreds of other tribes here was a puzzle, indeed, to the early explorers, but today there is no more mystery about it and the explanation of the possible means of such knowledge constitutes a part of our study.

We have been accustomed to think that man's first appearance in America was not many years before the coming of Columbus or the early explorers. I am speaking now of years in a relative manner, for a few hundred years, or a few thousand years, constitute a short time compared with the existence of the races of man. But the researches within recent years, by every department of geology and the study of man, have set back man's presence in America many thousands of years. Some years ago no one would have believed that human beings dwelt in America more than twenty thousand years ago. Today we have proof

that is indisputable that man not only inhabited
North America thousands of years ago, but that
the races of man existing in this country at that
time were the equal if not actually the superior of
the races of man in the old world at the same time.
I have in mind the exhibits from the gravel deposits
in Frederick, Oklahoma, and in Raton, New
Mexico, where we have seen articles that were
buried and associated with animals known to have
lived only in very ancient times. Such animals
were mastodons, camels, horses, elephants,
ground-sloths and others. Underneath the fossils
were found flint arrow-heads and spear heads and
other human-made articles, and some of these
were buried in the bodies of the animals and were
still attached to the bones of these animals who had
been killed with them, and these animals are indisputably and scientifically recognized as belong-
ing to very ancient periods. In at least fifty
localities in North America such exhibits have
been found. The most definite proof was found at
Colorado, Texas, where flint weapons which had
undoubtedly killed the animals were within the
skeletons or embedded in the bones. Every

scientist and profound student of the subject of the origin of man in America will tell you that the evidence is rapidly piling up and while some of these may not admit with me the existence of Lemuria as a separate continent with its own race of people, they will admit that people came to America many, many thousands of years ago from some unknown country in the west.

Chapter II.

FASCINATING INCIDENTS OF THE PAST

———

THE idea that there have been a number of continents which disappeared in ages gone by is very old and is found expressed in various ways in the oldest legends of many lands. There are references in many ancient writings to tribes of people living toward the east or toward the west in localities that are now occupied with seas and oceans.

I must avoid the subject of the continent of Atlantis as much as possible because that lost continent has been well dealt with in the book by Ignatius Donnelly and by others and because as a story, not as fascinating as that of Lemuria, would occupy a complete volume in itself. But, for many centuries the idea of a lost continent having once existed in the space now occupied by the Atlantic Ocean was expressed in hundreds of manuscripts and books, though considered often as merely a legend without scientific foundation. Even when Sir Francis Bacon wrote his famous book called "The New Atlantis" and thereby gave some weight to the old stories of a lost Atlantis, many still believed that the ancient continent was as mythical as the New World he described. Along with the coming of the realization that the new Atlantis described by Bacon was a prophetic picture of the United States and Canada, also came a realization, through scientific discoveries, that the lost Atlantis might be more fact than fable.

In recent years, however, all doubt about a submerged continent at the bottom of the Atlantic Ocean has been cast aside, for the great scientific explorations and tests have revealed that there is such a continent, and that at one time it undoubtedly filled most of the space between the shores of the New World and the Old World in the temperate zone. The Azores Islands and the Madeira Islands are now generally accepted to be mountain peaks of the ancient Atlantis continent still lifting their heads above the ocean's surface. That there were other such islands in the Atlantic in centuries gone by is now generally believed because of the many references to them in ancient writings.

The disappearance of the continent of Atlantis, however, is only one incident in the history of the changes that have taken place on the surface of this earth. It is more than likely that at one time there was far more land than water, and because of the picturesqueness of the subject I wish to deal lightly and briefly with some of the great changes that unquestionably took place. It is impossible in a book of this kind and in a limited chapter of this nature to speak of all of these changes in detail.

First of all, we cannot exactly determine how large the continent of Atlantis really was, but, of course, we can be sure it came in contact with North America and Africa. It may appear as though this would indicate that the continent of Atlantis must have been very large, but we will anticipate that argument by stating that there are other good scientific reasons for believing that the continental shores of North America as we know them today and the shores of the European coast were not as widely separated as at the present time. First of all we have evidence to show that the coast lines of both continents have been gradually changing, just as they are changing to-day. Despite the many places in which man has filled in, with earth and other material, various points and places along each coast and especially along the North American shore, the washing away of the earth and the disappearance of part of the land along the ocean has been more rapid and more exhaustive than we realize at first considera-tion. Many of the very ancient maps that show discrepancies between the present coast lines of North America and Europe are not the result of error, but fairly accurate pictures of what the coast line was at one time.

We have no reason to assume that a continent is something that is anchored and fastened to the center of a great sphere and is immovable. Small islands have shifted as well as disappeared and re-appeared in times past and it is possible for an en-tire continent to move either eastward or west-ward or even toward the north or south or twist itself slightly diagonally. Scientists now believe that because a continent can float and move on the surface of the earth that very likely the North